I0159042

Holiness
Jesus' Imminent Return

by Pastor Star R. Scott

**The doctrine of the blessed hope
is the greatest contributor to holiness.**

Star Publishing

Copyright © 2005 by Pastor Star R. Scott.

All rights reserved. No portion of this book may be reproduced, stored in a retrieval system or transmitted in any form or by any means - electronic, mechanical, photocopying, recording, or any other - without the written permission of the copyright owner. Published in Sterling, Virginia. Published by Star Publishing.

All Scripture quotations are from the King James Version of the Bible (KJV).

ISBN-13: 978-1-938520-09-9

Table of Contents

Publisher's Note

The work you hold in your hands is a compilation of sermon transcripts that Pastor Star Scott has delivered to his Sterling, Virginia congregation during 40 years of ministry there. While using segments of transcriptions is certainly not the most common format for a published work, the possibility of doing so was approached with care and deliberation.

In recent years, with the republication of older Christian literature, some publishers have taken considerable license in editing the writing of great authors who have since gone home to be with the Lord. This seems to have been done in the interest of making the writings more palatable for today's Christian reader. Because of our interest in maintaining the integrity of the doctrine and even retaining the anointing that was on these messages as they were originally delivered, we have decided to present them here in transcribed form.

Perhaps the most direct admonition to take this approach came from one of the great pioneers of the Pentecostal movement in the twentieth century, Willard Cantelon. Cantelon, who was truly an eloquent man, and mighty in the scriptures, considered Pastor Scott to be his spiritual pastor and dear friend. In a personal letter to Scott, Cantelon encouraged him: "I am sure that recording your sermons on tape is one of the 'wisest' things you do. And knowing that these messages can be transcribed in writing and find their way to the different 'levels' of readers in the days ahead is a long-range vision that is most real." In another letter, Cantelon continued by saying, "There is something special about what is delivered 'live' and printed the way it is given." We certainly agree with Brother Cantelon's perspective on these matters and therefore present these timely yet timeless teachings in such a format.

As you prepare for the soon return of our Lord and seek to strengthen your relationship with Father, we pray that you will be helped, challenged, and enriched by these teachings.

Holiness
Jesus' Imminent Return

**The doctrine of the blessed hope
is the greatest contributor to holiness.**

The Greatest Contributor to Holiness

"And every man that hath this hope in him purifieth himself, even as he is pure." (1 John 3:3)

The doctrine of the blessed hope is the greatest contributor to holiness. It's not how hard you try. It doesn't have to do with whether or not there is enough time in prayer or study. It doesn't have to do with self-discipline and, "Somehow I have to pull myself away from the cares of this world." I want you to understand that if you believe in the imminent return of Jesus Christ, you will live a holy life. It will absolutely provide all the external motivation that is necessary. How many of you, like myself, need external motivation, or are you so totally disciplined and internally motivated that you need nothing external? I think all of us need external motivation. We all need to understand that there are benefits and consequences to all our actions. These benefits and consequences direct us and are not purely internal motives.

To live expecting the imminent return of the Lord will keep your life sanctified. If you believe Jesus can come now, you will make the right decisions at every moment. He didn't come then, but He could come now! Living with the expectation of the blessed hope will feed into sanctified living—a godly lifestyle in this ungodly world. Clearly understand that the blessed hope, the expectation of the Lord's momentary coming, will cause a pursuit of sanctified living. I think, in Paul's theology, the rapture of the church was a great emphasis in the believers' daily sanctification. They remained sanctified as they expected Jesus to return. The blessed hope is the primary motivation for our holiness. I'm not saying that the blessed hope is the assurance of our escaping hell, which then motivates us to righteousness. The blessed hope, or the sure coming of the Lord Jesus Christ, motivates us through the appreciation of the free gift provided. We then understand the justice of God that's going to be met, the opportunity to see Him and to be like Him, and the opportunity to be free from the power of sin that still works in our members and holds us captive. It's an expectation of the finished work, the fulfillment, and the redemption of our bodies, the apostle said. It's a motivating factor, and it causes us to rejoice and to continue to press on and expect the imminent return and imminent deliverance from sin's power.

Everything that is going on in our lives is preparatory for this one moment. The sanctified life is evidence of the intensity of our looking for that blessed hope. Do you really believe that He is coming back? You'll know the effects of regeneration in your life by the fervency of your expectancy of the Lord's return. I'm not talking about you walking around, banging into poles because you're always looking up. I'm talking about an inward looking up, an expectation, and the fact that we're making our decisions based upon that.

The Treasures of the Sanctified

"For where your treasure is, there will your heart be also."
(Matthew 6:21)

We can judge our sanctification by how much we are in prayer, how much we are studying, and how involved we are in evangelism. Are we abstaining from the things that used to really hinder our lives, from the weights and the sins that did so easily beset us? Are we now free from some of those questionable activities that drew strength from our lives? Those are all good ways to analyze whether we're living lives that are sanctified, but look at the context of Titus, which says that grace instructs us to deny ungodliness. How do I know if I am denying ungodliness? How do I know if I'm free from worldly lusts? How do I know if I'm living soberly and righteously and godly in this present world, with everything bombarding me on a daily basis? One of the greatest ways to know whether you're living a sanctified life is by this thirteenth verse. Are you looking for that blessed hope, the glorious appearing of our great God and Savior, Jesus Christ? One of the greatest ways of knowing whether you're sanctified or not is by knowing where your treasure is. Where is your focus? What are you excited about today? Is it the return of the Lord? Can you say you're one of those people who loves His appearing, or, as the Scripture says, who is looking for Him? Hebrews 9:28 says, "...and unto them that look for him shall he appear the second time without sin unto salvation." Are you looking for Him?

I think it's time to have our hearts stirred up to look for that glorious appearing of the Lord Jesus Christ. How many of you are living momentarily expecting the Lord's presence? If you are, it changes the course of your life. You're not caught up with cares. You're not caught up with anxieties. You understand that we're just sojourners; we're just passing through. Nothing in this life is really what it's all about. It's about preparation for the coming of the Lord; and every man that has this hope will purify himself even as He is pure. If you believe the Lord's return is imminent, if you believe it's something that is immutable (it's sure; there is no change in the course of God), then you will make decisions for eternity, not for the moment. Whether your decision has to do with your vocation or the way you're going to respond to interpersonal relationships, the decision is made with the understanding that things can change in a moment, in the twinkling of an eye.

Changed into Father's Likeness

"Behold, what manner of love the Father hath bestowed upon us, that we should be called the sons of God...." (1 John 3:1)

How many times over the years have you heard that passage quoted? This is something that just burns in my heart and is a reality to me in understanding the love of God. How can we be sons and not long for His appearing? How can we be sons and not want to be with Dad and to be acceptable in His sight? How can we be sons of God having experienced His love, when we can't look on Him and say, "You know, I want to be like Him"? There is nothing greater than to have a son say, "I want to be like my dad." It has nothing to do with the natural, and, for those of us who are believers, it has nothing to do with any temporal acquisitions. It has nothing to do with ideology; we all pass that on because our children are being raised in that environment. The ideology is something that is transferred. But we as believers have one desire, don't we? It's that we could be an example, that we could turn to our children and say, "Follow me as I follow Christ." If you're comfortable with your pursuit of God, your desire is to be able to hear a son say, "I want to be like Dad. I want to be able to

5

pursue God. I want to know that Jesus is the preeminent factor in my life."

I'm not talking about during adolescence, but when our children were old enough to understand, it was made very clear to them that they were not number one in our lives. My children are not number one in my life; my wife is not number one—and it is clearly understood that I am not number one in their lives.

"Behold, what manner of love the Father hath bestowed upon us...." Only when Jesus is Lord and everything else is in proper order are you free to love freely. There is nothing more rewarding than hearing a son say, "I want to be like Dad and make Jesus number one." That is what this passage is all about.

One of my favorite Bible teachers of all time, a pastor who had as much influence on my life as anybody, was Kenny Schmidt. He was one of the great teachers on prophecy and pastor of one of the first super-churches in the nation. Referring to California, he said, "This is God's handiwork, where the mountains kiss the sea, and we're in the middle of the big smack." This area of the country is gorgeous, but its beauty is all a shadow in comparison to looking on His face. God's handiwork is seen in the greatest sunsets, the greatest peaks, the beauty of the desert in full bloom, Yellowstone and the Grand Tetons, and the majesty of the Great Lakes. But His glory so far exceeds these beautiful things, making them only a shadow. They don't even begin to express the glory of what we will feel when we look on Him. Even if we could put a whole lifetime of experiencing these blessings together, it wouldn't even take a moment. It couldn't even begin to have the effect that one glance of His eyes and one glimpse of His face could have on our hearts. Come quickly, Lord Jesus! The blessed hope is the glorious appearing of the great God and our Savior, Jesus Christ.

Expectation for the Imminent Return

"But of that day and hour knoweth no man, no, not the angels of heaven, but my Father only." (Matthew 24:36)

There is to be a constant expectation and preparation for this hour in which we're living. Although the hour of His return isn't known, you need to live with the immediate return on your heart. The hour isn't known, but the hour is now. If it is imminent, it's now. This is the hour—not necessarily the hour that He is coming, but the hour that you need to be ready. This is the hour, right now, that you need to be ready because He may come. Though we don't know the hour, we do know the standard of preparation, and it's immediate.

The Lord's return is imminent. The Scripture tells us that nobody knows the day or the hour. What we do know is that He has gone to prepare a place for us; and if He has gone and prepared a place, He'll come again and receive us unto Himself, that where He is there we may be also (John 14:2-3). We need to prepare our lives and to be watchful in the hour that's upon us. Make sure that all the weights and sins that can so easily beset us don't hold us down and blind our eyes. The god of this world constantly tries to blind our eyes with all of the things that glitter and that the flesh would delight in. Those things choke the Word of God out of our lives. What are we doing in our watchfulness? What are we doing to prepare ourselves, to make sure that we don't fall asleep? It is sooner than when we first believed. His coming, the Scripture tells us clearly, is at hand. We need to understand God's faithfulness as it pertains to His promises. The promise is that He is coming, and we realize in 2 Peter 3:9 that "the Lord is not slack concerning his promise, as some men count slackness." The promiseof God is that He will come again; Revelation 22:20 says, "Behold, I come quickly." We have the assurance of the Lord's coming, but some would say, "So, He is coming, but it's been 2000 years." But a day is with the Lord as a thousand years. You see, we're dealing with an eternal God. We're dealing with a God who is compassionate and loving, a God who sees the beginning to the end. We don't know how long His plan is going to continue. Nobody knows the day or the hour, but we can discern the seasons.

"But of the times and the seasons, brethren, ye have no need that I write unto you. For yourselves know perfectly that the day of the Lord so cometh as a thief in the night" (1 Thessalonians 5:1). He told them in this first epistle that His return was imminent. It's coming as a thief; nobody knows for sure when this hour will be. "Ye are all children of light [you've received this promise - the teaching, the illumination, the understanding that its imminent]. Therefore let us not sleep as do others; but let us watch and be sober." (verses 5-6). Don't get caught up in the cares of this world and the deceitfulness of riches. Don't become an earth dweller. Let

9

your eyes continually be looking up, for your redemption is drawing nigh. Don't be like the five foolish virgins that the Lord spoke of in Chapter 25 of Matthew, but keep your lamps lit and your vessels full.

Survey your own heart. Can you truly say, "I'm confident that I am not an earth dweller. I know who my first love is. I know in whom I have believed. I am persuaded that He's able to keep that which I've committed unto Him against that day, the day of the Lord"? The day of the Lord begins with the catching away of the church and continues through the millennial reign. Where are you? If the thief had come at midnight, would you have been ready?

Watching is Preparing

"Watch therefore: for ye know not what hour your Lord doth come. But know this, that if the goodman of the house had known in what watch the thief would come, he would have watched...." (Matthew 24:42-43)

Do you think you would watch if you knew the Lord's return was really close? It is! You can't get closer than imminent, at any moment! We must not believe it's imminent, then. Well, how do we believe it? We spend time in prayer and study. We understand the war that is going on for our souls and the strong delusion that is already in the world. The spirit of iniquity is already at work, and many of us are already being lulled to sleep. Well, what is God going to do about it? God has already done what He is going to do about it. He gives us all things that pertain to life and godliness in Christ Jesus. The Holy Spirit indwells us. The Word of God has been fulfilled and finished. It has provided for us, and the Lord ever makes intercession for us. What are you going to do to be ready? The Scripture says if the man had known, he would have been ready, and his house wouldn't have been broken into.

"Watch therefore, for ye know neither the day nor the hour wherein the Son of man cometh" (Matthew 25:13). How many

11

of you think maybe we ought to get a little more diligent in our daily watching? How many of you can look back on last week and think that maybe you let a day or two slide by when you weren't focusing on the coming of the Lord? Your decisions and your life's course were being directed by natural cares rather than by the spiritual awareness of your being a sojourner and citizen of heaven.

We're not to be caught up, like the rest of this world, in what's going on here in the temporal realm. Our hearts and our minds are intent on the fact that each day we're serving for the eternal purpose of the glorification of our Lord and the kingdom of God. At a day when you think not, the Son of man comes. Now, we don't know what hour He is coming, but the one thing we do know for sure is that He is coming, amen? That's what's exciting. You hear these words, but in reality what are you doing to prepare yourself? In trying to be as truthful as you know how to be with your own heart, you must ask yourself what really takes priority in your life. You can lie to everybody else, but you can't lie to yourself. You can say all the right words. You can quote the doctrine. You can defend your case—"I'm doing these things because God told me to; God's leading me," or whatever you want to say—but His Word has already established your course. Your responsibilities have been defined, and the whole issue is whether you are a doer of the Word rather than being just a hearer and a parrot. "Every man that has this hope in him purifieth himself even as He is pure." How tragic it will be for those of us who are not only unprepared but are causing others to stumble. It would be better for a millstone to be tied around our necks. There will be an even greater judgment for those who don't do these things and who teach others to be disobedient. Watch therefore, for you know neither the day nor the hour when the Son of man comes.

Where are you today in your preparation for the coming of the Lord? Has anything distracted you? Have the cares of this world, the deceitfulness of riches, the lust of other things distracted you? How about the pursuit of that new job? How about looking for that husband or that wife? How about looking toward graduation day at school? What is the joy of your heart? What takes your time and energy? I'm not saying that any of those things are wrong. I'm asking if any of those things dilute your craving for the first love, the hunger and thirst for the coming of the Lord Jesus. The Scripture says He's going to appear to those that love His appearing, not to those who say, "Oh man, there it is. I had something planned. Well, okay. I'll come, Lord."

We see that there is a lot of false doctrine, a lot of demonic power and deception in this age in which you and I are living. This is a day of great prosperity, and men are lovers of pleasure more than lovers of God. This is a day of great religion. We talk about great revival in America. Some people would think we're having another Great Awakening, but it is nothing more than entertainment programs. We're trying to imitate the world and doing a poor job of it, and people are coming out for fifteen-minute sermons. People are talking religion, but denying the power to live holy lives. They deny the infallibility of the Scriptures. We have to be very aware of what's going on around us; we must know those that labor among us and are over us. The Scripture says to be imitators and followers of those who through faith and patience are inheriting the promises of God. We're all given that admonition to guard ourselves, to be sober, and to be watchful.

Loving Jesus' Appearing

*"So Christ was once offered to bear the sins of many; and unto them
that look for him shall he appear the second time without sin unto
salvation." (Hebrews 9:28)*

The Scripture says He's going to appear to those that are looking for Him. How many of you can say you were looking for Him today? The Scripture says He's going to come and appear to those that love His appearing. What are you doing to get a better eyeshot? What have we done to take away all the cloudiness, or, as the apostle says, the "weight, and the sin which doth so easily beset us"? What have we done to strip ourselves for this race so that we could be free and strong and fresh in our pursuit of this great promise of the coming of the Lord? He is coming for those that are looking for Him, those that have made the preparation. What are we doing? If we love His appearing, we will prepare. It's the expectation of our hearts. At any moment that trumpet can sound. The dead in Christ will rise; those of us who remain shall be changed in a moment, in the twinkling of an eye, the Scripture tells us.

Do you love His appearing and look for that visitation? It is the hope of the church, and we can be assured that one of these days we're going to hear the trumpet of God sound and hear the words "Come up hither!"

Where do you find yourself in this great day that we're living? The hour is coming on us. How do you find yourself today? Are you lighter? Do you feel like you almost don't even have to have the trumpet sound? Are you so light, because the cares and weightsare so minimal, that you're ready for take-off? How heavy do you find yourself today?

The bride is supposed to be making herself ready. What about the bride that leaves you standing and waiting at the altar? She was in the back getting ready, but it has been an hour and a half, and you're still standing there. She comes in and says, "Well, a few friends said there was a sale down at the mall. There was this cute little pair of shoes that were really to die for." The answer to that whole thing is, "Yeah, and you're not to die for." It's obvious where that heart is. I know this is hypothetical, but you wouldn't wait an hour and a half. I sure wouldn't! The Lord doesn't wait a moment. There's no waiting. He calls; you come. If you don't have the right garments, you can't enter in. If the oil is not sufficient, you can't enter in and there is no second chance. Watch therefore!

Do You Love Me More Than These?

"So when they had dined, Jesus saith to Simon Peter, Simon, son of Jonas, lovest thou me more than these?" (John 21:15)

Jesus asked the question after the miraculous supply, "Do you love Me more than these?" That's the question being asked here. God is not blessing us by the jobs we possess, the positions we occupy, or the neighborhoods we live in, for us to consume it upon ourselves. He has placed each of us strategically in different parts of society to reach this world with the message of the gospel of Jesus Christ. We are to let them know that He's coming soon and that free access has been given to them by the blood of Jesus Christ. Are we about His business? Do we love His appearing, or are we caught up in the mundane? Where are our lives? Can we say as the apostle said, "For me to live is Christ"? That's the only reason I exist. The crown of righteousness is for those that love His appearing.

We're talking about the rapture of the church. We're talking about who's going to go. Not everybody who says "Lord, Lord" is going. Not everybody who says he is a Christian is going in the rapture. You must love His appearing. This brings comfort and hope. It'll take away depression, and it'll destroy apathy. It'll create an anticipation of your Lover's arrival, and a last-minute preparation for the day you'll finally see Him and rush into His arms. "To those that love His appearing…"

Can you envision a soldier returning home after fighting in World War II without anyone at the dock to greet him? Finally he makes his way back to his apartment, opens the door, and finds his wife lying on the couch in her curlers, watching television. She says, "Glad you're home. There's a TV dinner." There's no love there. You stand on the dock, waiting for the boat. You see this little speck on the horizon, and, finally, this massive vessel brings your treasure. A sea of faces pours off the gangplank, but you can only see one. Your eyes meet, and your heart leaps. How much anticipation is there for Jesus' return?

In Matthew 25:21 the words are spoken, "Well done, thou good and faithful servant: thou hast been faithful over a few things, I will make you a ruler over many things: enter thou into the joy of thy lord." The treasure that awaits us is the joy of His presence alone. There is one way to find out if you're going to obtain that eternal joy. Does His presence cause joy? Does it satisfy you? Are you looking for something else? Is your satisfaction in a person, a spouse, a child, a thing, or a possession? If He's not your first love, then He's not your only love. He will have no other gods before Him. This is a powerful word that is given to us.

It's Not Enough To Be Holy

"For the grace of God that bringeth salvation hath appeared to all men, Teaching us that, denying ungodliness and worldly lust...."
(Titus 2:11-12)

Titus tells us that we are to look for the blessed hope. We are to look for it; there is nothing automatic in that. I want you to see the statement Titus makes concerning the blessed hope that is before each one of us. The context of the second chapter is the preparation of our lives in holiness: "Teaching us that, denying ungodliness and worldly lusts, we should live soberly, righteously, and godly, in this present world" (Titus 2:12). In the same breath, the Holy Spirit talks about our own personal sanctification and holiness in these last days. He says it is not enough just to be sanctified; it is not enough just to be holy. He says that to live godly in this world will cause you to look for "that blessed hope, and the glorious appearing of the great God and our Saviour Jesus Christ" (verse 13).

The words in Titus 2 are really the culmination of this hope and excitement in the hour that we're living, based upon the grace of God. We're going to fail in our own strength. We're not able to see, in our own imaginations, what's going on in our midst. We're hindered in the natural; but the Scripture says

19

we're not blind, and that day will not overtake us unaware. Those who are walking in the Spirit have spiritual eyes to see what is really going on behind the scenes in this hour. Are you aware of what's happening around you? Are you aware that sometimes all of those great "blessings" may be Satan's delusion to destroy you? Could the person whom you believe the Lord brought into your life actually be somebody who is drawing you away from the fire that once burned in your heart?

We can say, "Well, the Lord said that it's not good for man to be alone, so He provided spouses." We stand for that principle. What I'm trying to point out to you is that many times what we think are blessings—things that God has said are lawful for us—are diluting our hearts if God is not the source. You need to ask yourself if this person spiritually enhances your life. I'm talking to some of you singles and young adults right now. Don't ask if it is lawful or if they are a believer. That is not the issue. He or she can be a believer, but is this person going to cause you to pursue more of the kingdom of God, or is this person going to want more attention drawn to himself, diluting your pursuit? These are all very real questions we have to deal with. God sends people into our lives primarily to sanctify us, to refresh us, and to strengthen us. That is why it is not good for us to be alone. Two are better than one—if it's two with the same zeal and fervency in their hearts.

Now, beloved, many of us today are faced with little piddly temporal worries, trials, and pressures. I want you to understand something clearly: Jesus is coming! There is no financial pressure, no transgression made against you, no squabble in your marriage, no dashed hope or dream, no prejudice, no separation from the politically or economically elite in this world who snub you so that you cannot get in with the "in" crowd, that can cause you to lose your hope.

Living Godly in this Crummy Old World

"Teaching us that, denying ungodliness and worldly lusts, we should live soberly, righteously, and godly, in this present world."
(Titus 2:12)

We've talked much about the call to sanctification and the grace that enables us to walk free from sin's power. There is no true biblical grace without the consequence of having a pursuit of holiness, a denial of worldly lusts; but one other thing has to accompany that. We could possibly think that we're free from worldly lust because we're not engaged in "gross sin." We're not involved in things that are an obvious abomination, but look what he goes on to say. "I want you free from worldly lusts. I want you to live godly in this present world." Being godly is not just a moral condition; being godly is divine dependence. A godly life is not only a divine dependence on God for everything—not just morality, not just sanctification—but it's also godly affection.

"For the grace of God that bringeth salvation hath appeared to all men, teaching us that, denying ungodliness and worldly lusts, we should live soberly, righteously, and godly, in this present world." The grace of God teaches us that we should live soberly, righteously, and godly right now in this crummy old world. Therefore, grace doesn't teach us that God is going to overlook our lascivious lifestyles. The grace of God teaches us that (through the blood of Jesus, the indwelling power of the Holy Spirit, and the abiding Word of God in us, which is a lamp unto our feet) we are capable of walking free from ungodliness and worldly lusts, and we can live soberly, righteously, and godly in this present world. How many of you lived godly today? Thank God for it.

Now, how do we pull off this walk in the Spirit that would cause us to live this kind of sanctified life? We live this type of lifestyle with what anticipation? Look at verse 13: "Looking for that blessed hope, and the glorious appearing of the great God and our Saviour Jesus Christ; Who gave himself for us, that he might redeem us from all iniquity, and purify unto himself a peculiar people, zealous of good works. These things speak, and exhort, and rebuke with all authority. Let no man despise thee." We're looking for that blessed day of the coming of our Lord Jesus Christ. The blessed hope is that at His return, old things will have truly passed away and all things will have become new, because at His appearing (the Bible says in 1 John) we will see Him as He is, and we will be like Him. Aren't you looking forward to that day? The Bible makes it very clear that corruption will take on incorruption in that day; mortality will take on immortality, praise God! The coming of the Lord will be an exciting time!

This doctrine is despised by earth-dwelling Christians. They're concerned that we're not as caught up with the temporal things as they are. We're not looking to lay up treasures for ourselves on earth; we're looking to lay up treasures in heaven. The context of this passage in Titus has to do with sanctified living. It has to do with what our real treasures are. It has to do with the fact that we can live differently than the world in the midst of all of these temptations and the draw that the world's system has upon us. It's the grace of God that enables us. What causes it is the constant looking for that blessed hope. You can't live a sanctified life without the doctrine of the imminent return of the Lord being prominent in your life. It's impossible. You will be overcome. You will be brought down by the weights and sins if there's not a constant looking up and expectation of the coming of the Lord.

The Consistency Factor

"Be ye also patient; stablish your hearts: for the coming of the Lord draweth nigh." (James 5:8)

James established two virtues here: patience and consistency. Be patient. Don't get in a hurry, but at the same time be consistent in your godliness (in your practical living), allowing your hearts to be established, strengthened, solidified, and purified. Why? "...For the coming of the Lord draweth nigh." It's near. It's sooner than when we first believed.

Patience and consistency are two factors necessary in the preparation of our hearts. Be patient, consistent, and constant in your preparation. It's going to be a discipline. The world wants us to live selfishly for the moment. All that is within man has to do with hoarding, fear, and taking thought for the morrow: "What am I going to eat? What am I going to drink?" All of these are natural within fallen man because of his need to live by the sweat of his brow and to persevere in his own strength. James says that those of us that are redeemed, who are part of the kingdom, can't live by that law anymore. We are to seek first the kingdom of God and His righteousness, and all of these other things will be added unto us.

Don't let anything hinder you; don't let any man steal your crown. Why? Because the coming of the Lord is drawing near, sooner now than when we stirred our hearts last. What have we done in those days? How seriously aware are we of the imminent return of the Lord Jesus? You see, the one thing about the doctrine of imminence is how it affects our lives in preparation to soberness, to not let that day come upon us unaware. Realize, as it says in Thessalonians, we're not children of darkness; we're in the light. We've received the revelation of the imminent return of the Lord, and, because of that, there will be constant preparation. Our watching is to be momentary; our preparation is to be constant. That's the admonition the Lord has given us.

We need to look practically at our lives. We can say all we want about our expectation of the Lord's coming. "I'm believing that Jesus is coming back." I know there are extremes in the minds of some men. Some would sell all they have and want to sit around and wait for the coming of the Lord, while others would forsake everything and do thus and so. Then if the Lord happens to tarry, there they are. There are extremes to both sides, and you need to discern where your heart is in this matter. James says, "Be patient; stablish [settle] your hearts." Know what it is that you really believe. Don't deceive yourself. Look inside and find out what the treasure of your life really is. Know what you are preparing for, because the Lord said in Revelation 3:11, "Behold, I come quickly: hold that fast which thou hast, that no man take thy crown." He is coming quickly, so hold fast. Don't let any man take your reward from you. Don't be seduced by the world's system.

Worldly Cares that Choke Our Holiness

"And take heed to yourselves, lest at any time your hearts be overcharged with surfeiting, and drunkenness, and cares of this life, and so that day come upon you unawares." (Luke 21:34)

Very frankly, every one of us is vexed on a daily basis, and the sins and weights that do so easily beset us affect every one of us. Every day that we go into this environment, we are affected. Every time we step out of our prayer closet, every time we enter the world, we're defiled. It's filthy out there. The world heaps weights upon us. We carry out the sin in our members that loves all that the world offers. The flesh's appetite loves it, craves it, and wants to identify with it. We walk as new creations that keep our members under, that reckon ourselves dead indeed unto sin and alive unto Christ.

What do you do to cleanse yourself and to take off these weights that have been put upon you from the day's activities? If you've lost your first love, you're not spending time purifying yourself as He is pure, or in preparation because you love His appearing. The things of this world just continue to weigh you down, and now you've lost your joy and peace; you've lost your desire for the Word, and prayer is now just something that's scheduled in. His presence isn't the only thing that brings you satisfaction. There's not a willingness to sell all that you have to obtain the pearl of great price. When was the last time you prayed, "Come quickly, Lord Jesus"? People are just getting a little bit too comfortable with this life's existence. The treasures have now become the house, family, possessions, and vocation. Do you know Him? Has your life's course changed? Is your treasure in the heavens? Is His presence your joy and your strength—the only thing that satisfies you?

How much has the world influenced what we really believe and how we apply it in our daily walk? How has the spirit of lawlessness affected you and me in our looking up for the coming of the Lord? Have we become earth dwellers and lovers of pleasure and ease in this life so that we've lost sight of the imminent return of Jesus Christ in the rapture? Does it occupy your thoughts daily, moment by moment? Do you understand that we're just pilgrims here passing through? This world is not our home. Come quickly, Lord Jesus! How strong a hold do all of those temporal things have on you—the fact that you may be getting married, the new job, the new house, the new baby, whatever it is? Those things in life that are so often rewarding to us are, in and of themselves, no problem: but have they occupied our minds so much that we've lost our vision, our hunger, our desire, or our passion for the return of Jesus?

What Thoughts Consume You?

"Be careful for nothing; but in every thing by prayer and
supplication with thanksgiving let your requests be made known
unto God." (Philippians 4:6)

There are some of you who are saying, "I believe the Lord is coming," yet your mind right now is running off to all the little cares and hassles you went through today. You may have gotten crosswise with somebody at work or home, things are not right, you are under pressure in dealing with the kids, the finances are tight. Jesus is coming! We need to understand that all of these things (yes, they have to be dealt with) cannot consume you. Do not let that be where your thoughts or where your treasures are. Do not think upon those things; think upon things that are true and lovely, things that are pure. "Be careful for nothing; but in every thing by prayer and supplication with thanksgiving let your requests be made known unto God" (Phil. 4:6). This is what God has called us to.

What value have you placed on what God has called you to? How distracted are you by all the things you're involved in? When this gospel was first preached, there weren't the distractions and clatter that there are today. You know, when the day consisted of sitting on a mountain, throwing a few rocks at some sheep to get them to go in the direction you'd like, you had a lot of time to meditate. Your day may have consisted of just walking around, picking up stones, setting them on a wall, and building a boundary. Maybe you were walking behind a yoke of oxen, but the radio wasn't playing, and people weren't cutting you off on the freeway.

One of the hallmark cries of the church today is, "Come into our seminar, and we will give you peace of mind. We'll cause you, the church, to know how to abide in peace and cope with all of the pressures of life." There are little how-to formulas for being successful. I've shared this with you before. If you go into the bookstores today, you'll find books on how to cope with the pressures of life, but try to find books on sanctification. You can't find them. You can't find books on holiness or on the coming of the Lord. They're not there. I want to tell you something: if you want to learn how to cope and be successful in this life, then you're going to have to learn how to commune with God through the Holy Spirit rather than being an earth dweller. As long as your heart cares for the things of this world, you're going to be uptight. There are not enough tranquilizers, get-rich-quick schemes, or books like *How to Be Rich Without Really Trying, Think and Grow Rich, I'm Okay, You're Okay [They're Okay, Everybody's Okay]*. Godliness with contentment is great gain, and we need to return to that if we're going to know the peace of the Lord.

Keeping a Sanctified Life

"Beloved, now are we the sons of God, and it doth not yet appear what we shall be: but we know that, when he shall appear, we shall be like him; for we shall see him as he is." (1 John 3:2)

We need to ask ourselves if we're looking up and loving His appearing. It's not a fuzzy feeling; it's preparation. A lot of people get all sentimental and fuzzy during the holidays. That's not what it's all about. It's not about those feelings. It's about preparation. It's about working to make sure that we and our households are ready to enter that "ark," a type of preservation for the people of God in the moment of His justice and judgment.

Have you been having trouble keeping your life sanctified and orderly lately? Have you tried to pray a little bit more because you realize things are starting to get out of control? Are the cares of the world starting to weigh you down? Are the things you used to be free from trying to take hold of your life again? Are you thinking you need to pray and study a little more? Let me encourage you in one other approach. Why don't you start meditating on the return of the Lord? Why don't you start making your daily decisions based upon a momentary judgment, a momentary appearance of the Lord? Set your course in light of His imminent return, realizing that alone is the blessed hope. We continue to pursue and purge ourselves so that, as John says, we'll see Him one day. And when we see Him, we'll be like Him. This truth has been lost in many other doctrines.

We need to watch and pray. We need to have our lamps ready and our vessels full, amen? It isn't sufficient to have just enough to fire up our lamps. We must have enough to sustain us for the whole walk. Take time this week, and until the Lord comes, to spend in prayer and fellowship with the Lord through the Word. Let Him begin to refresh your spirit. Be strong in the Lord and in the power of His might. The Scripture tells us not to be drunk with wine, but to be filled with the oil of the Holy Ghost, amen? This is what the requirement is, so begin to exercise yourself to be more diligent in preparation for the coming of the Lord in these last days.

Moderation in the Temporal

"Let your moderation be known unto all men. The Lord is at hand."
(Philippians 4:5)

One of the things that causes us not to be ready is our life getting out of balance. If we begin to move excessively in one way or another instead of in the kingdom of God—if the worship and ministry that's due the kingdom is lacking— then we will not be prepared. There will always be things that will try to become excessive in our lives. God has called us to moderation, to seek first the kingdom of God with all of our hearts.

We experience so much busyness in this life. Knowing the prosperity and abundance that we have as a nation, we must ask ourselves what this life of moderation is. When does something become excessive in our lives? Whenever anything has replaced Jesus as our priority, as being preeminent, as being all in all, we have gone outside a life of moderation. Whenever anything robs us to the point where we digress—when the kingdom of God is not receiving what God has called us to place into it—then we've lost the standard of moderation. Have you taken seriously this admonition on moderation as it pertains to all that's temporal? We're in the world through moderation, but we're not of the world. We're seeking zealously; we're pressing on toward the mark, the prize, the high calling of God, with all our strength in preparing for things that are eternal. That's the admonition that's been given to us. "The Lord is at hand."

Children of Light Are Children of Truth

"Ye are all the children of light, and the children of the day: we are not of the night, nor of darkness. Therefore let us not sleep, as do others; but let us watch and be sober." (1 Thessalonians 5:5-6)

We are the children of day, the children of light; we are not of the night or of the darkness. Those people slumber, but we are to be watchful and sober. "For they that sleep, sleep in the night; and they that be drunken are drunken in the night" (1 Thes. 5:7). This is a reveling spirit. "Night" speaks here of something revealed in the next verse: these people prefer darkness. We're the children of light. We love light. We want the truth. Can you handle the truth? Can you handle the truth about your spouse? Can you handle the truth about your children? Can you handle the truth about your own heart? Are you comfortable in the light? Are you comfortable when people bring you reproof and instruction in righteousness "that the man of God may be perfect and throughly furnished unto every good work" (2 Ti. 3:17)? Do you read the Word of God to proof-text your own course, or do you let the Word be the mirror that reflects your soul, that protects you from forgetting what manner of man you really are? Children of light are truth seekers. I'm not talking about seeking the truth for everybody else, thinking you are setting everybody else straight and are the conscience of God. I guarantee you that everybody here has a full-time job taking care of himself.

We're called to walk in this light. We are referred to as "children of light." We don't have to get into the light; we are in the light. If Christ is in us, we are already the light of the world. We walk in truth and project the truth. We are the light of the world and the salt of the earth. The quest of heralding this gospel to the lost should consume us. It should be our passion to have somebody look upon us and see the light, and for others to say, "You're different."

Guardians of Our Homes

"But know this, that if the goodman of the house had known in what watch the thief would come, he would have watched, and would not have suffered his house to be broken up." (Matthew 24:43)

A s we look at the topic of the Lord's return, we're going to emphasize watchfulness, sobriety, and every one of us being ready. As I look over the congregation here, I realize the awesome responsibility we each have as heads of homes, and that I, as an overseer of this flock, will answer to God for whether or not we've done everything possible to make you ready. It's been our life's work to see a people whose hearts are prepared—a remnant that could be presented by the Lord to Himself, a holy church without spot or wrinkle or any such thing. That's our desire and what we long for, and it needs to be something that each one of us takes to his own heart, especially those of us that oversee households and others for whom we're going to answer. One of these days, we're going to stand and give an answer for everything in which we've labored to prepare for His coming.

I would like to ask you men, as it pertains to your house, are you watching? Is the thief ready to break in and steal the hearts of your wife and children? Has the world been allowed in and the blessed hope lost? We have to be prepared constantly. Can you say right now, "My house is ready; we're ready. Let the strong man come. Let the trumpet blow," or will you tragically say, as the words of that song, "I wish we'd all been ready"? "But God will give us another chance. He's a merciful and longsuffering God, not willing that any should perish." No, there won't be any second chances.

Are you making decisions based upon a temporal increase in goods and ease of life, or is the fact that we're just pilgrims here a reality? When I'm involved in things outside the pastoral ministry, this is the message that I take. This is the message of the gospel. The gospel is not a universal salvation in which Jesus died and everybody is going to be saved. It's when He comes and finds them doing. What's really important? What really sets the course of your life?

Are you an earth dweller, or is your treasure set above? Have you died to self? Are you going to be one that stands and says, "Lord, I cast out devils in Your name. I preached. I studied the Word of God. I witnessed"? He says, "I never knew you. You were doing it out of obligation. You were doing it out of fear. You were doing it out of pride. You were doing it from an intellectual perspective of what Christianity is, but you never gave Me your heart." The falling away will only be of those who've chosen not to abide. If you've chosen to abide, you'll do His commandments, not your own. You can't set your own agenda and operate within the kingdom of God. The King determines the action of each of our lives. Where are you now? I trust that you're abiding in the Vine. I trust that you're laboring in the vineyard as He's appointed. I trust that day will not overtake you. Break up the fallow ground; it's time to seek the Lord.

The Vexation of the Disorderly

"And the Lord direct your hearts into the love of God, and into the patient waiting for Christ. Now we command you, brethren, in the name of our Lord Jesus Christ, that ye withdraw yourselves from every brother that walketh disorderly...." (2 Thessalonians 3:5-6)

Contextually, I believe this is saying for us to withdraw ourselves from those who aren't expecting the return of the Lord. They will pollute and vex you. Not all men have faith to believe that Jesus is coming back. "There's going to be a church that doesn't believe in My return, and they'll pollute your life."

"For [you] yourselves know how ye ought to follow us: for we behaved not ourselves disorderly among you" (2 Thess. 3:7). Here Paul is speaking about the idleness and deception that were taking place. We've talked about what this disorderly behavior is. It's ob-vious that he's speaking here to those who are not living in the pursuit of the blessed hope. Many people have rejected this doctrine. He said, "You have to understand that they're going to influence you in a negative way and rob you of your hope." And they could, as said in Revelation 3:11, "take thy crown." Don't let any man steal your crown. You have to finish this race. Whom are you investing your time and energy into?

The more you believe in the return of the Lord, the more you'll gather together with believers. Church won't be something you have to do; it'll be something you get to do. You get to come and comfort and stir up your heart and your expectation of the coming of the Lord Jesus. How can we better affect those that God brings into our lives than by being here as His agents to propagate this gospel? I believe that the Holy Spirit has ordered us into this area again as a way of preparing our hearts so that we don't fall into the slumber of a Samson, or judge ourselves by our intentions while not living for, or like we believe in, an imminent return.

Holy Harvesters

"He that goeth forth and weepeth, bearing precious seed, shall doubtless come again with rejoicing, bringing his sheaves with him."
(Psalm 126:6)

Another thing that the belief in the imminent return of the Lord will do to you is to cause you to be an evangelist. It'll cause you to share freely what you've received rather than rushing through life without being concerned with those that are being damned. How can they hear without a preacher? What is important to tell them: where that big sale is; where you got that bargain; how they can buy this stock; how they can beat the system in this way? What are we spending our time telling people? It's all going to burn up, amen? The weights and sins, the destroying forces of strong delusion and prosperity, and the spirit of iniquity are already at work. Have you seen professed Christians whose eyes are already blinded? Come quickly, Lord, and save us.

His Second Coming becomes the major doctrine that motivates us in hastening the return of the Lord. It motivates us to go into all the world and preach this gospel as quickly as possible, and to put our full effort into being epistles that are read of men. It motivates us to be the light of the world and the salt of the earth. All of this runs in direct correlation to how we believe and whether it's part of our doctrine. If we believe in the coming of the Lord Jesus Christ, it will motivate our lives in every one of these areas.

Do you want to be a part of the harvest? I'm looking forward to it. It's not enough just to share and have our own lives ready to be harvested. The Scripture says that we are to bring some sheaves with us in preparing to meet the Lord in the air. The judgment seat of Christ will follow. All of our works are going to be judged and tried by fire, the Scripture says. Each one of us needs to prepare himself to appear before the Lord. There's nothing greater than to be able to stand before Him and hear the words, "Well done, good and faithful servant," and then be able to look around and see people that are in His presence because of your faithfulness. Is it worth what it's going to cost us to finish this race for one soul? I think it's worth it to forsake all and follow Him, not only for you, but also for the one who is there because you were faithful. I think it's beyond measure. There's nothing that will compare to your being able to look over and see one person that made it because you did your job. Think about it. That's what our task is here. We need to be busy about His business.

Consecrating the Mundane Areas of Life

"...Nevertheless when the Son of man cometh, shall he find faith on the earth?" (Luke 18:8)

We approach everything we do from an eternal perspective. What makes the mundane, or the temporal, have an eternal effect? Consecration. We take the mundane and consecrate it to God. Our lives are wholly consecrated to Him. We are about our Father's business. "When the Son of man cometh, shall He find faith on the earth?" the Scripture asks. When He comes, will He find you representing Him on the job? Are you looking for His coming? Do you look to Him as the One who will elevate you on the job so that you don't have to backbite, undercut others, and vaunt yourself, but are just humbly serving and looking to glorify God? Don't push yourself ahead, but let God, in His own wisdom, place you in a way that would not rob from your family or from the community of believers; for God makes us rich and adds no sorrow with it. You'll know if it's God who makes you rich. If God is the One who's promoting you, it will not cost the kingdom of God. It will not take away from the household of faith. It will not take away from your family or cause any compromise in your life. It will not cause any compromise of character or pursuit. When we go on the job, we're able to tell if God is making us rich by living our lives to honor Him.

The Need to Have Excess Oil

"And the foolish said unto the wise, Give us of your oil; for our lamps are gone out." (Matthew 25:8)

Is it taking every bit of spiritual energy you can muster just to get through the day, just to keep from backsliding? Your oil is not sufficient. There needs to be an excessive presence of the Holy Ghost in our lives, amen? There needs to be an excess of oil. There need to be rivers of water welling up and overflowing in us, praise God. It's not just enough of Jesus to get me through the day. We don't know how many days are ahead. We don't know the strength that we must draw upon to make us to stand. The wise took sufficient oil—not only enough for the lamp, but enough in their vessels.

Have you come to hate your flesh? Have you really come to grips with how vile you are? Do you enjoy your life without the awareness of how needy you are to be glorified? It's one thing to walk in sanctification, but sanctification is a shadow of glorification. It's nothing compared to what we're going to be. I don't know about you, but I'm so looking to be changed, praise God, and to have corruption take on incorruption, and mortality take on immortality. Are you pretty content? Are you satisfied with the way things are going? "You know, it's not that bad. I'm walking free from the power of sin better than I ever have, praise God. God is blessing me: I'm feeling pretty good in my body, I'm prospering, things are going well, the house is in order, and things are looking pretty good!" Is there an earth-dwelling mentality there? Are you content, or are you homesick for the better—the glory of God? When you look on His face, as the old hymn says, do "the things of earth grow strangely dim in the light of His glory and grace"? Loving His appearing, watching, and looking for Him have to do with this transfer of treasures, as we saw in Luke. Where are the treasures, really, in your life? What is it that satisfies, and what is it that you're looking toward?

Here we are, as dull as the Laodicean church, rich, and have need of nothing! "...I would thou wert cold or hot. So then because thou art lukewarm...I will spue thee out of my mouth" (Rev. 3:15-16). People have trouble understanding why the Lord said He would rather us be cold. You see, cold is identifiable. At least you know you are cold. Lukewarm is deception; lukewarm is mingled seed.

These things that I am speaking to you will break a hard heart. His Word is like a hammer that breaks the rock in pieces. If you have a heart of flesh, it should move you to say, "Dear God, I'm so thankful I've been set right. Lord, just stir me to go share with others." That's what a heart of flesh says. A heart of stone is either broken or dull of hearing. It hears and says, "Yeah, yeah, but I've heard this before. I've tried and haven't been able to change anyway, so what's the difference now? Yeah,

I've heard about the Lord's coming, but everything remains as it is." God said that would happen to the dull of hearing. He said that Satan comes immediately and steals the word out of our hearts because of the shallowness of the ground (Mark 4:15). We've just been too busy tilling other ground, making provision for the flesh, and setting our own course.

Do Something About Your Apathy!

"And if thy right eye offend thee, pluck it out, and cast it from thee: for it is profitable for thee that one of thy members should perish, and not that thy whole body should be cast into hell." (Matthew 5:29)

Are we ready for the Lord's coming? If not, let's do something about it! You may be sitting here now and saying, "Man, the weights and sins that do so easily beset us have dragged me down. The cares of this world, the deceitfulness of riches, and the lust of other things have entered in and choked the Word of God out of my heart. I'm strangling. I know I'm not right. I know I've lost the zeal for God. I know that I don't have my first love. I know that I'm lukewarm." Then do something about it! If your eye offends you, pluck it out; if your hand offends you, cut it off! Do you understand that the consequence of not being ready is eternal damnation? If you believe that, you'll change. If I could hold the fire up against you, if I could somehow reveal to you the real wrath of God—the torment of hell, the rejection of God, darkness, total loneliness, screaming yet not being heard, your name being forgotten, no one ever knowing or caring that you existed—and could truly convince you that you were going to enter into that state in the next fifteen seconds if you didn't change, how many of you think you'd change? The real issue is, you don't believe it! You just don't believe it, that's all. You can say you believe, but faith without works is dead!

"I've said, 'Jesus is Lord,' but He's not really Lord. He's kind of an addendum to my life. I kind of have Him there for a time of crisis. And if there is a hell, I'd really like to escape it. I try to be moral, and I just can't bring myself to say the Bible is not the Word of God, but I'm not going to change." Now, you don't say that; you just don't change. And you didn't change last week, and you didn't change last month, and you didn't change last year. Why not change today? Why not let the Word of God enter your heart and change you today, bringing regeneration and re-creation? Why not allow the lordship of Jesus its place in your heart now?

If you look at your own heart and are not excited about the coming of God, you are in danger. All I can share with you is that you are in grave danger, and making a public profession will not change it. It will not be done in five minutes. There are some that are in jeopardy. Let this Word break your heart now. Cry out to Him for the grace and mercy that's available to you. Watch it all die; watch it all fall before you and count it as dung that you might win Christ. Watch your will dissolve and His lordship become a reality. You need to fall on your face before God. If it takes all night, you need to stay on your face until you have been broken, until your treasures have become the eternal, until your prize is the high calling of God in Christ, until you see Him. Every ounce of your energy will be spent in preparation to know that you know Him, so that you can say, "Come quickly, Lord Jesus." Make it your heart's prayer, in Jesus' name.

Pour Out Your Heart To Him

*"He which testifieth these things saith, Surely I come quickly.
Amen. Even so, come, Lord Jesus." (Revelation 22:20)*

B egin to pour your heart out to Him, saying, "Lord, I'm making time to watch and pray. That day will not take me unaware. I'm making provision to seek the Lord. I purpose in my heart to do the Word of God. Help me, Lord. I can't believe unless You give me the grace and the faith, and I ask You to help me believe." When we stand in His presence, He'll reward every one of us according to our works. The Bible says that as He rewards us for all those works that He enabled us to participate in, we'll take those crowns and cast them at His feet, saying, "Holy, Holy, Holy!" He's all in all. Don't you want to see Him? Don't you want to be like Him and know Him as He is? Then prepare yourself; purify yourself; cleanse yourself. Look up; your redemption is drawing nigh.

We rejoice in the fact that the Holy Spirit is effecting the washing of the water of the Word by our Husband in us right now, preparing us so He can present us to Himself. We don't present ourselves; He presents us to Himself. If we're going to try to present ourselves, then it's going to burn up. We are totally dependent. We can't do anything to appease God or to merit anything from God. It's all His righteousness, it's all faith and grace, and it's recognizing the vanity of self-reliance and worth. We are absolutely, one-hundred percent dependent upon Jesus' redemption to make us right with God. The works don't make us right. The failures don't make us unworthy. We so long to see You, that we might be like You.

O Lord, we want to be a people whose hearts yearn for Your coming. We pray, "Come quickly, Lord Jesus!" You're going to appear to those who are looking for You, to those who love Your appearing. Help us to be watchful, sober, not caught up in surfeiting and the cares of this world and the deceit of riches, but seekers of the kingdom first. Help us to be seekers of righteousness, lovers of lost souls, ministers to the body of Christ, defenders of sound doctrine, a bride making herself ready. O Lord, it's our desire. Lord, it's our desire that we would be ready, that we would have sufficient—more than enough— to fill the lamps of our hearts. We know where to get the oil, Lord, that we would have sufficient. That day is coming when every knee will bow and every tongue will confess that Jesus is the Lord. Make it your confession now, and you'll be ready.

Waiting Patiently

"For our conversation is in heaven; from whence also we look for the Saviour, the Lord Jesus Christ." (Philippians 3:20)

We hear stories of brothers and sisters, from the Coliseum in the first century to those of twentieth-century China, who were persecuted. We've heard stories about people being confined in little four-by-six boxes but never losing the joy of the Lord. It was because of the doctrine of the imminent return of the Lord. It was because of their patient waiting. They believed that at any moment, their deliverance was at hand. Would they be found faithful when Jesus came?

"I go and prepare a place for you," and "I will come". I wonder if during the torment of Mao and Idi Amin, that's what sustained the believers as they were tortured and imprisoned. I wonder if the return of the Lord isn't what gave them their strength and their belief, knowing that He could come at any moment and bring His judgment and that even if they died, to be absent from the body is to be present with the Lord. To partake of that martyr's crown would give them preeminence in the resurrection, because "the dead in Christ will rise first."

How easy is it for you to say under your breath, "Well, I might as well just quit," because you stubbed your toe somewhere in business? I had to take a ten-dollar-an-hour cut. It's a whole different perspective when you see the purification that's in the church worldwide, and historically, what the body of Christ has been subjected to. Our eyes are not to be on the comfort zone of daily life, but on the eternal presence of God and His imminent return and this promise to those who patiently wait. Oh, beloved, we've talked so much in the last couple of years about the rocking of a people to sleep in this nation through our affluence. We've quoted the scripture, the eschatological scripture, that says, "And Antichrist will destroy them by their prosperity." This secret power of lawlessness pervades every area of our lives. Are we aware of the hour and the jeopardy that we're in? Are we patiently waiting with our eyes fixed on the heavens? Is that where our conversation is? Can we say it's in Him alone that we live, move, and have our being? This doctrine affects so many areas of our lives, and we have the promise that He's coming.

Father, we ask You to purify us. Lord, give us grace and strength to make ourselves ready as the bride of Christ. We confess You as the Lover of our souls. We say that we love You, but too often we live for ourselves or others. We know the washing is by the water of the Word alone. We can have great intentions, but we have to spend time in Your Word to be clean and refreshed. Strengthen us with Your Word, and cause us to hope in it and to boast in the great promises. For that which is working effectually in each one of us, we just say, "Thank You." Cause us to lift up our eyes as though we'd just seen You ascend, saying, "I'll return for you." Help us to look up, for surely our redemption is drawing nigh. Help us to be ever ready, ever watching, hoping, and loving Your appearing. Make it real, Father, in Jesus' name. Amen! Hallelujah!

www.ingramcontent.com/pod-product-compliance
Lightning Source LLC
Chambersburg PA
CBHW060716030426
42337CB00017B/2893

* 9 7 8 1 9 3 8 5 2 0 0 9 9 *